KETO CHRISTMAS

COOKBOOK

A
Collection of the Best Keto Recipes
For
Christmas

CARLY GOODHART

Copyright

Carly Goodhart © Copyright 2020 – All rights reserved.

Except as permitted under the U.S. Copyright Act of 1976, the contents contained in this book may not be duplicated, reproduced, or transmitted without the prior written permission of the author or the publisher.

Under no circumstances will a legal responsibility or blame be directed towards the author or the publisher for any monetary loss, reparation, or damages based on the information in this book, directly or indirectly.

Disclaimer Notice:

Note that it is important that the following information contained in this book is for educational purposes only. After carrying out enough research work, we present a piece of detailed and accurate information as it relates to the present norm. We got the contents in this book from various sources, and hence, the intending readers are not given a warranty. We advise readers to talk to their licensed doctors before trying out the techniques given within this book.

By consenting to this document, the reader accepts that the author is not responsible for any loss either directly or indirectly that can be incurred as a result of the information contained within this book, and also the omissions, errors, or inadequacies of the reader.

Table of Contents

KETO CHRISTMAS 1

COOKBOOK 1

LENORA SAWYER 1

COPYRIGHT 2

TABLE OF CONTENTS 3

KETOGENIC DIET 5

BROILED SALMON 8

CREAMY TUSCAN CHICKEN 10

CAJUN PARMESAN SALMON 13

LEMON GARLIC SHRIMP 16

AIR FRYER STEAK 18

ROASTED TURKEY 20

KETO MEATLOAF 23

TUSCAN BUTTER SALMON 26

KETO MEATBALLS 30

GARLIC ROSEMARY PORK CHOPS 33

ROAST BEEF 35

BEEF TENDERLOIN 37

BACON-WRAPPED TURKEY 41

KETO RECIPE WITH SAUTÉ LEMON CHICKEN WITH GREEN BEANS 44

KETO DIET WITH SALMON FISH CAKES WITH DILL SAUCE 47

KETO RECIPE WITH SALMON CURRY 50

KETO RECIPE WITH CHIMICHURRI LAMB STEAK WITH COCONUT CREAMED CAULIFLOWER MASH 53

KETO RECIPE WITH LAMB PHO WITH ZUCCHINI NOODLES AND POACHED EGGS 56

AIR FRYER ASPARAGUS 59

BACON WRAPPED TURKEY BREAST WITH TOMATOES RECIPE 62

LOW-CARB CANDIED YAMS WITH MARSHMALLOWS 64

KETO MASHED CAULIFLOWER 68

KETO PECAN PIE CLUSTERS ... 72
KETO CORNBREAD ... 75
KETO PUMPKIN PIE ... 77
KETO SCALLOPED TURNIPS ... 80
LEMON GARLIC SALMON ... 83
MINI PUMPKIN CHEESECAKE TARTS ... 88
LOW-CARB RASPBERRY BAKED BRIE ... 92
ROASTED BRUSSELS SPROUTS SALAD WITH MUSTARD BASIL VINAIGRETTE ... 95
PERFECT DEVILED EGGS WITH BACON ... 98
KETO PUMPKIN SEED BREAD ... 103
SLOW COOKER PUMPKIN CHEDDAR SOUP WITH CHORIZO ... 105
STUFFED PORK TENDERLOIN AND ROASTED RADISH ... 108
SWEET 'N TANGY CRANBERRY RELISH ... 112
ROASTED TURKEY LEG ... 114
EASY GARLIC BUTTER HERB ROASTED TURKEY ... 117
LOW CARB CREAMED SPINACH WITH CREAM CHEESE ... 121
CONCLUSION ... 124

Ketogenic Diet

A keto diet is soundly branded for being a low carb diet, where the body emanates ketones in the liver to be for energy. It goes by many various names: low carb diet, low carb high fat, ketogenic diet, etc.

When you take in a food substance with high carbs, your body system will manufacture insulin and glucose.

- ***Insulin*** is manufactured for processing the glucose in your bloodstream by taking it around the body.
- ***Glucose*** is the simplest molecule for your body to convert and use as energy so that it will be chosen over any other energy source.

Since the glucose is being used as a primary energy, your fats are not needed and are therefore stored. Typically, on an average, higher carbohydrate diet, the body will use glucose as the primary energy source. By lowering the intake of carbs, the body is induced into a state known as ketosis.

To start a keto diet, you will want to plan. That means having a viable diet plan ready and waiting. What you eat depends on how fast you want to get into a ketogenic state (ketosis). The more restrictive you are on your carbohydrates (less than 25 grams net carbs per day), the faster you will enter ketosis.

The ketogenic diet for weight loss is grounded on the impression that driving the body into the ketosis phase will exploit fat loss. Ketosis is a normal metabolic process that occurs when the body does not have enough glucose stores for energy.

When these stores are depleted, the body resorts to burning stored fat for energy instead of carbs. This process produces acids called ketones, which build up in the body and be used for energy.

Here are the benefits of keto diet

    a. Helps with weight loss

    b. Helps get good level of cholesterol

    c. Can help in reducing blood pressure

    d. Aids in brain disorders

    e. Heart diseases

    f. It helps in reducing seizures

    g. Acne

    h. Anti-inflammatory

    i. Helps fight cancers

    j. Migraines

Above is a little information about Keto Diet.

Happy reading! Enjoy your Christmas!

Broiled Salmon

Yields: 4 Servings Overall Time: 20 Mins

Recipes:

- One tablespoon of Grainy mustard
- Four salmon fillets (4-oz.)
- One tablespoon of finely minced shallots
- Two cloves garlic (finely minced)
- Kosher salt
- Two teaspoons of fresh rosemary (chopped)
- Half lemon juice
- Lemon slices (serving purpose)

- Two teaspoons of fresh thyme leaves (chopped, add more for garnish)
- Freshly ground black pepper

Directions

1. Heat up the broiler and line a baking sheet with parchment. In a small clean container, mix together, garlic, mustard, thyme, shallot, lemon juice and rosemary and season with pepper and salt. Spread mixture all over salmon fillets and broil, seven to eight minutes.
2. Garnish with lemon slices and extra thyme and serve.

Creamy Tuscan Chicken

Yields: 4 Servings Overall Time: 40 Mins

Recipes:

- Four boneless skinless chicken breasts
- One tablespoon extra-virgin olive oil
- Freshly ground black pepper
- One teaspoon of dried oregano
- Kosher salt
- Three tablespoons of butter

- Three cloves garlic (minced)
- One and a half cups of cherry tomatoes (halved)
- 1/4 cup of freshly grated Parmesan
- Half cup of heavy cream
- Lemon wedge (serving purpose)
- Three cups of baby spinach

Directions

1. In a clean skillet over medium heat, heat up oil. Add the chicken and season with pepper, oregano and salt. Afterwards, cook until appears golden and not pink anymore, eight minutes for each side. Take out the skillet and put aside.
2. Melt butter in the same skillet over medium heat. Stir in the garlic and cook until begins to fragrant, approximately one minute. Add cherry tomatoes and season with pepper and salt. Cook until

tomatoes are starting to burst, add spinach and then cook until spinach is starting to wilt.

3. Stir in parmesan and heavy cream and bring mixture to a simmer. Decrease heat to low and simmer until sauce is slightly compact, approximately three minutes. Take the chicken back to skillet and then cook until heated through, five to seven minutes.

4. You should then serve with lemon wedges.

Cajun Parmesan Salmon

Yields: 4 Servings Overall Time: 45 Mins

Recipes:

- Four fillets salmon ((4-oz.) preferably wild)
- One tablespoon of extra-virgin olive oil
- Freshly ground black pepper
- One tablespoon of freshly chopped parsley, plus more for garnish

- Two tablespoons of butter
- 1/3 cup of low-sodium chicken or vegetable broth
- Two teaspoons of Cajun seasoning (divided)
- One lemon juice
- Lemon slices (serving purpose)
- Three cloves garlic (minced)
- One tablespoon of honey
- Two tablespoon of freshly grated Parmesan

Directions

1. In a large clean skillet over medium to high heat, heat up oil. Season salmon with pepper and one teaspoon Cajun seasoning, then add to the skillet with the skin side up. Cook salmon until it appears extremely golden, approximately six minutes, flip and then cook two mins additional. Move to a plate.

2. Add garlic and butter to skillet. When butter has melted, stir in lemon juice, broth, remaining teaspoon Cajun seasoning, honey, Parmesan and parsley. Bring mixture to a simmer.
3. Decrease heat to medium and add salmon back to skillet. Simmer until sauce has compact and salmon is well cooked, three to four mins more.
4. Add lemon slices to skillet and then serve.

Lemon Garlic Shrimp

Yields: 4 Servings Total Time: 15 Mins

Recipes:

- One tablespoon of extra-virgin olive oil
- Two tablespoon of butter (divided)
- One lemon (thinly sliced) plus one lemon juice
- One-pound medium shrimp (peeled and deveined)
- Three cloves garlic (minced)
- Kosher salt

- One teaspoon of crushed red pepper flakes
- Freshly chopped parsley (garnish purpose)
- Two tablespoons of dry white wine (or water)

Directions

1. In a large clean skillet over medium heat, melt olive oil and one tablespoon butter. Add lemon slices, shrimp, crushed red pepper flakes and garlic, and season with some salt. Cook, occasionally stirring, until the shrimp appears pink and opaque, approximately three minutes for each side.
2. Take away from heat and stir in left over butter, white wine and lemon juice. Season with salt & garnish with parsley before serving it.

Air Fryer Steak

Yields: 2 Servings Overall Time: 45 Mins

Recipes:

- Two cloves garlic (minced)
- Four tablespoons of butter (softened)
- One teaspoon of freshly chopped chives
- Two teaspoons of freshly chopped parsley
- One teaspoon of freshly chopped rosemary
- One teaspoon of freshly chopped thyme
- Freshly ground black pepper

- One (2-pounds) bone-in ribeye
- Kosher salt

Directions

1. In a small clean container, combine herbs and butter. Place in middle of a piece of plastic wrap and roll into a log. Twist ends together to keep airtight and refrigerate until solidifies, twenty mins.
2. Season steak on each side with pepper and salt.
3. Put steak in basket of air fryer and cook at 400 degrees Fahrenheit for twelve to fourteen mins, for medium, depending on thickness of steak, flipping halfway through.
4. You can top steak with a slice of herb butter to serve.

Roasted Turkey

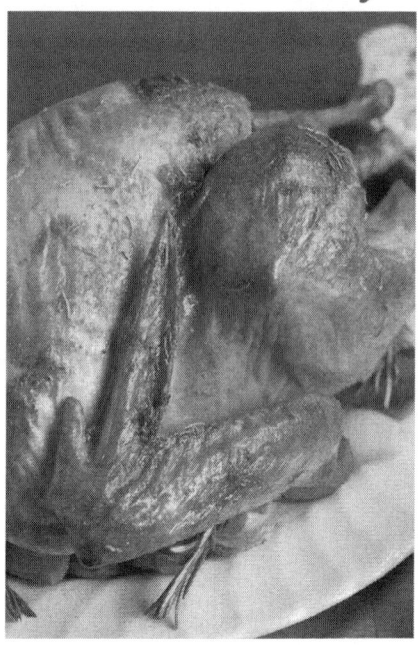

Yields: 8 Servings Overall Time: 3 Hours 15 Mins

Recipes:

- Kosher salt
- One (14-pounds) whole turkey (neck & giblets removed)
- One onion (cut into wedges)
- Freshly ground black pepper

- One bunch of thyme
- Two cups of chicken broth
- One small handful sage leaves
- One small handful of rosemary sprigs
- Half cup of melted butter
- One head garlic (halved crosswise)

Directions

1. Place rack to the lower third of the oven and heat up the oven at 450 degrees Fahrenheit. Using a paper towel pat dry the turkey and season the cavity with enough pepper and salt. Stuff the cavity with thyme, onion, sage, garlic and rosemary. Using a kitchen twine, tie the turkey legs and tuck the wing tips under the body.
2. Use butter to coat the turkey then season with enough salt and pepper. Place the turkey breast side

up on a roasting rack inside of a large clean pan. Transfer chicken broth into the pan. Then place into oven and cook for thirty minutes, then decrease oven heat to 350 degrees Fahrenheit.

3. With the juices on the bottom of the pan, baste every thirty to forty-five minutes, and then roast for three to four hours, or until the juices run clear when you cut between the leg and thigh.

4. Using an aluminum foil cover cooked turkey and let it cool for twenty minutes before starting to carve.

☐

Keto Meatloaf

Yields: 6 Servings Total Time: 1 Hour 15 Mins

Recipes:

- One tablespoon of extra-virgin olive oil
- One stalk celery (chopped)
- One medium onion (chopped)
- One teaspoon of dried oregano
- One teaspoon of chili powder

- Three cloves garlic (minced)
- 1/4 cup of grated Parmesan
- One cup of shredded cheddar
- Half cup of almond flour
- Two-pounds ground beef
- One tablespoon of low-sodium soy sauce
- Six thin strips bacon
- Kosher salt
- Freshly ground black pepper
- Two big eggs
- Cooking spray

Directions

1. Heat up oven to 400 degrees Fahrenheit. Grease a medium baking dish with cooking spray. In a medium skillet over medium heat, heat oil. Add onion and celery and cook until soft, 5 minutes. Stir in garlic, oregano, and chili powder and cook until fragrant, 1 minute. Let mixture cool slightly.
2. In a large bowl, combine ground beef, vegetable mixture, cheese, almond flour, Parmesan, eggs, soy sauce, and season with salt and pepper. Shape into a large loaf in baking dish, then lay bacon slices on top.
3. Cook until bacon is crispy and beef is cooked through, about 1 hour. Cover dish with foil, if bacon is cooking too fast.

Tuscan Butter Salmon

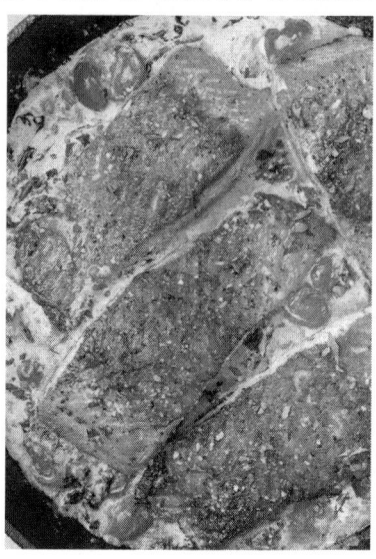

Yields: 4 Servings Overall Time: 45 Mins

Recipes:

- Four (6-ounce) salmon fillets (patted dry using paper towels)
- Two tablespoons of extra-virgin olive oil
- Freshly ground black pepper
- Kosher salt

- 1/4 cup of chopped herbs (such as parsley), additional for garnish
- Three cloves garlic (minced)
- Three tablespoons of butter
- Two cups of baby spinach
- One and a half cup of halved cherry tomatoes
- Half cup of heavy cream
- Lemon wedges, for serving (if desired)
- 1/4 cup of freshly grated Parmesan

Directions

1. Heat up oil in a large clean skillet over medium to high heat. Season the salmon with pepper and some salt. As soon as oil starts shimmering but not smoking, add salmon but the skin side should be up and cook until appears totally golden,

approximately six minutes. Turnover and then cook for two minutes more. Move to a plate when done.

2. Decrease heat to medium and then add butter. As soon as butter has melted, stir in garlic and then cook until it begins to fragrant, approximately one minute. Add cherry tomatoes and then season with pepper and some salt. Cook until tomatoes are starting to burst, and then add spinach. Cook until spinach is starting to wilt.

3. Stir in Parmesan, herbs and heavy cream and then bring mixture to a simmer. Decrease heat to low and simmer until sauce is slightly compact, approximately three minutes.

4. Take the salmon back to skillet and spoon over sauce. Simmer until salmon is well cooked, approximately three minutes additional.

5. You should garnish with more herbs and squeeze in lemon on top before serving it.

Keto Meatballs

Yields: 4 Servings Total Time: 50 Mins

Recipes:

- For The Meatballs:
- One clove garlic, minced
- One-pound ground beef
- Two tablespoon of extra-virgin olive oil
- 1/4 cup of freshly grated Parmesan, plus more for serving

- Half cup of shredded mozzarella
- One large egg (beaten)
- Two tablespoon of freshly chopped parsley
- Half teaspoon of freshly ground black pepper
- One teaspoon of kosher salt

For The Sauce:

- Two cloves garlic (minced)
- One medium onion (chopped)
- One teaspoon of dried oregano
- One can crushed tomatoes
- Freshly ground black pepper
- Kosher salt

Directions

1. In a large clean container combine garlic, beef, Parmesan, mozzarella, egg, parsley, pepper and salt. Make into sixteen meatballs.
2. Heat up oil, in a large clean skillet over medium heat. Add meatballs and then cook, occasionally turning, until appears golden on each sides, approximately ten minutes. Take away from skillet and put on a paper towel-lined dish.
3. Add onion in same skillet and cook until it becomes soft, five minutes. Add garlic and cook until begins to fragrant, one minute additional. Add oregano and tomatoes and season with pepper and some salt.
4. Add meatballs back to skillet, cover and simmer until sauce has thickened, fifteen minutes. You should the garnish with Parmesan before starting to serve.

Garlic Rosemary Pork Chops

Yields: 4 Servings Total Time: 30 Mins

Recipes:

- Kosher salt

- Four pork loin chops

- One tablespoon of freshly minced rosemary

- Freshly ground black pepper

- Half cup of butter (1 stick)(melted)

- One tablespoon of extra-virgin olive oil
- Two cloves garlic (minced)

Directions

1. Heat up oven to 375 degrees Fahrenheit. Season pork chops generously with salt and pepper.
2. Mix together garlic, butter and rosemary in a small clean container. Put aside.
3. Heat up olive oil in an ovenproof skillet over medium to high heat, then add pork chops afterwards. Sear until it appears golden, four minutes, turn and cook for four minutes additional. Coat pork chops with garlic butter.
4. Transfer the skillet in oven and then cook until it is well cooked, ten to twelve minutes. You can serve with more garlic butter.

Roast Beef

Yields: 8 Servings Total Time: 2 Hours 10 Mins

Recipes:

- 1/4 cup of extra-virgin olive oil
- One round roast (4-lb.)
- Three cloves garlic (minced)
- One tablespoon of chopped fresh rosemary
- One teaspoon of freshly ground black pepper

- Two teaspoon of kosher salt

- One tablespoon of chopped fresh thyme leaves

Directions

1. Heat up oven to 450 degrees Fahrenheit. In a small clean container, combine garlic, oil, thyme, rosemary, pepper and salt. Use to coat the roast.

2. On a roasting rack, place roast in roasting pan. Roast for fifteen minutes, then decrease heat to 325 degrees Fahrenheit and roast for one hour forty minutes additional, or two hours for it to be well roasted.

3. Take away from the oven and let it cool for fifteen to thirty minutes before serving it.

Beef Tenderloin

Yields: 4 Servings Overall Time: 1 Hour 50 Mins

Recipes:

For Beef:

- Two tablespoons of balsamic vinegar
- Half cup of extra-virgin olive oil
- Three sprigs fresh thyme
- Three sprigs fresh rosemary
- Two tablespoons of whole grain mustard

- Two cloves garlic, smashed
- One bay leaf
- 1 (2-pound) beef tenderloin
- Two tablespoons of honey
- One teaspoon of kosher salt
- One teaspoon of dried rosemary
- One clove garlic, minced
- One teaspoon of freshly ground black pepper

For Yogurt Sauce:

- One teaspoon of freshly ground black pepper
- Half cup of Greek yogurt
- 1/4 cup of sour cream
- Kosher salt
- Horseradish (prepared)
- Half lemon juice

Directions

1. In a large clean container, mix together vinegar, oil, thyme, mustard, bay leaf, rosemary, honey and smashed garlic. Add meat to container, cover with plastic wrap, and marinate in refrigerator for 1 hr or up to one day.

2. Heat up oven to 450 degree Fahrenheit. Using aluminum foil, line a rimmed baking sheet and fit a wire rack inside. Take out tenderloin from marinade and then using paper towels, pat dry. Season with pepper, salt, minced garlic and rosemary, then place on rack.

3. You can roast as you desire, approximately twenty minutes. Let it cool, five to ten minutes before slicing.

To make sauce:

1. In a medium clean container, whisk together sour cream, yogurt, lemon juice and horseradish, and season with salt afterwards.
2. Serve with sauce on the side and slice the tenderloin.

Bacon-Wrapped Turkey

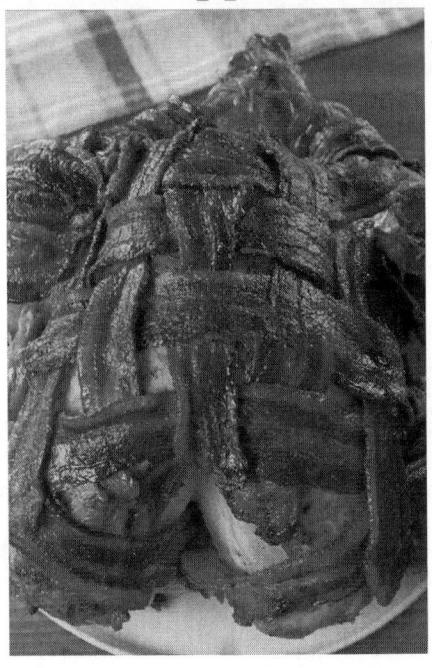

Yields: 12 Servings Total Time: 3 Hours 10 Mins

Recipes:

- One large red onion (cut into large wedges)
- One (11-lb.) turkey (neck & giblets removed)
- One bunch of rosemary
- One bunch of thyme
- One teaspoon of chili powder

- Half cup of melted butter (1 stick)
- One teaspoon of kosher salt
- Half teaspoon of garlic powder
- One-pound bacon
- Half teaspoon of paprika

Directions

1. Heat up oven to 375 degrees Fahrenheit. Stuff cavity with thyme, rosemary and onion, then tie legs her and tuck wings in.
2. In a medium clean container, stir together the seasonings with the melted butter. Brush turkey all over with butter mixture.
3. Transfer the turkey in a clean roasting pan. Place strips of bacon on turkey & weave together.
4. Bake for three hours, or until an instant read thermometer inserted into the thigh records 165

degrees. After 2 hours check and cover with foil if bacon becomes too dark.

⬚ Keto recipe with Sauté Lemon Chicken with Green Beans

Estimated time for preparation is 10 minutes

The time to conclude cooking is 20 minutes, and it can be served twice.

Recipes:

For Sauté Lemon Chicken:

- Three tablespoons of lemon juice (45ml)
- Four cloves of garlic (12g)
- Chopped medium onion 0.5 sizes (55g)

- Two diced chicken breasts (400g)
- One tablespoon of tamari sauce
- Pepper and salt for seasoning
- Chopped 0.25 cup of parsley (4g)
- Two tablespoons of ghee (30ml)

For Green beans:

- Four cloves of garlic (12g), either diced or minced
- Chopped green beans (168g)
- Two tablespoons of avocado oil (30ml)
- Pepper and salt for seasoning
- A tablespoon of tamari sauce

☐Directions

1. Kindly add avocado oil in a pan (preferably non-stick) and sauté green beans with garlic and tamari sauce.

2. Then, add ghee and stir fry garlic and onions until they soften in the same pan.
3. Then you can add the diced chicken to the same pan and keep stirring for 6 minutes. If necessary additional ghee is optional
4. Then add lemon juice, parsley, and tamari sauce to the chops. Constant stirring is required until the chicken is cooked, then you can season with salt and pepper. Then serve

Keto Diet with Salmon Fish Cakes with Dill Sauce

Estimated time for preparation is 10 minutes

Time to conclude cooking is 25 minutes, and it can be served twice

Recipes:

For Salmon Fish cakes:

- Two medium whisked eggs.
- A tablespoon of well chopped fresh dill (3g)
- Two cans of salmon (340g)

- 1/8 cup of coconut oil (30ml)
- 1/8 cup of Shredded Coconut (10g)
- 1/8 cup of coconut flour (7g)

For Cooking The Fish Cakes:

- Two (2) tablespoons of coconut oil (15 ml)

Creamy Dill Sauce:

- 1/8 cup of mayonnaise (30ml)
- One clove of garlic either minced or diced (6g)
- 1/8 cup of coconut milk (30ml)
- A chopped teaspoon of fresh dill (1g)
- Pepper and salt for seasoning

Directions

1. Kindly combine all the dill ingredients and whisk. Then the dill sauce will be served with salmon fish

cakes. In the case of excess sauce, it is advisable to preserve by refrigeration.
2. Then all the ingredients from the fish cakes should be combined to form four (4) patties.
3. Kindly melt 15ml of coconut oil in a pan (preferably non-stick) then carefully place the patties in the hot oil.
4. Cook the other side until its golden brown (about 4 minutes also) then serve.

Keto recipe with salmon curry

Estimated time for preparation is 5 minutes

Time to conclude cooking is 10 minutes, and it can be served twice

Recipes:

- Green beans (196g)
- Diced fillets of salmon (2)
- Chopped fresh basil (2 tablespoons)
- 120ml of coconut cream
- Coconut oil (2 tablespoons)

- Chicken broth (2 cups i.e., 480ml)
- 55g of medium diced onion
- Garlic powder (1 teaspoon)
- Curry powder (one and a half teaspoon) and pepper and salt for seasoning.

Directions

1. Kindly melt coconut oil in a saucepan, then add sauté and onions until it becomes radiant. This process should take up to 3-4 minutes.
2. Then add green beans to the saucepan, and while doing that, add sauté to the green beans for up to 6 minutes.
3. Increase the heat temperature too high. Add broth to boil with it.
4. Add curry powder, garlic powder, and salmon to the saucepan and continue to boil for up to 1 minute.

5. At this point, you can reduce the heat to simmer and stir in the coconut cream.
6. Continue to simmer for 5 minutes until the salmon is cooked.
7. At this point, you can add salt and pepper to taste.
8. Partition the curry between 2 bowls and sauce with basil leaves.

Keto recipe with Chimichurri Lamb Steak with Coconut Creamed Cauliflower mash

Estimated time for preparation is 15 minutes

Time to conclude cooking is 20 minutes, and it can be served twice

Recipes:

For the steak:

- Four lamb steaks
- Two tablespoons of ghee

For Coconut creamed Cauliflower mash:

- Head of cauliflower smashed into small florets (300g)
- Two tablespoons of ghee

For the Chimichurri Sauce:

- Half cup(8g) of chopped parsley
- One chili pepper (14g)
- Three tablespoons of olive oil
- One tablespoon of lemon juice
- Two teaspoons of apple cider vinegar
- Six cloves of garlic (18g)
- Pepper and salt for seasoning

Directions

1. The chimichurri sauce can be made by blending all the ingredients of the chimichurri sauce. In case of any leftover, it's advisable to refrigerate.

2. Get a frying pan to fry the steaks with two tablespoons of ghee until desired.

3. To make the cauliflower mash, its advisable to boil the cauliflower. Then place the cauliflower, salt, and ghee in a blender. Additional coconut milk or ghee is needed if desired is not met. In case of any leftover, it's advisable to refrigerate.

4. Serve the steaks with an equivalent amount of chimichurri sauce and Coconut creamed cauliflower mash.

Keto recipe with Lamb Pho with Zucchini Noodles and Poached Eggs

Estimated time for preparation is 10 minutes

Time to conclude cooking is 15 minutes, and it can be served twice

Recipes:

- Two bulbs of green onion
- One full lemon chopped into four wedges
- Four eggs

- Two lamb steaks (chopped into chunks)
- Two zucchinis
- Ten tablespoons of fresh basil leaves.
- A teaspoon of cinnamon powder
- Two cups of chicken broth or soup.
- Half tablespoon of freshly grated ginger. Then pepper and salt for seasoning

Directions

1. Boil and poach four eggs in a pot.
2. Put the broth in a pot and start heating. As soon as the broth starts boiling, add ground cinnamon and grated ginger and pepper and salt.
3. Slowly add the lamb chunks into the broth and ensure that they are not glued together.
4. Keep cooking until the lamb chunks are adequately cooked.

5. Partition the peeled, boiled eggs in the middle of two large bowls and divide equally between the two large bowls.
6. Then peel the zucchinis and use a spiralizer to produce zucchini noodles.
7. Serve with lemon wedges.
8. Two wedges per person.

Air Fryer Asparagus

Yield: 4 Servings Overall Time: 15 mins

Recipes:

- One pound of Asparagus
- One tablespoon of either Olive Oil or Avocado Oil
- Half teaspoon of Sea Salt
- One tablespoon of either Butter or Ghee (melted)

- Two tablespoon of Coconut Aminos
- One tablespoon of Balsamic Vinegar

Directions

1. The ends of the asparagus stalks should be trimmed. Afterwards each asparagus stalk should be cut into halves. Asparagus can be put in a clean container or bowl with a lid then shake, You can also brush oil on the asparagus or a ziplock bag can be used to confirm it's equally coated. Then, Sprinkle with sea salt.

2. The asparagus should be mixed in the clean basket of the air fryer. Then, cook for approximately ten minutes at 400 degrees, but thinner stalks of asparagus might take just about 8 mins.

3. Prepare your sauce while cooking the asparagus. Mix together balsamic, butter and coconut aminos

4. Pour the sauce on the prepared hot asparagus then serve to enjoy!

Notes

Tamari Soy Sauce can be used instead of coconut aminos if not instead in a Paleo Diet.

Bacon Wrapped Turkey Breast with Tomatoes Recipe

Yields: 4 Servings Overall Time:6 hours 10 minutes

Recipes:

- One pound of raw turkey breast
- 8 oz of pre-sliced bacon (thinly cut)
- Three tomatoes (ensure it is diced without skin)
- Half teaspoon of garlic powder

- Half teaspoon of <u>black pepper</u>
- <u>Salt</u> (has desired)
- <u>Bay leaves</u> (has desired)

Directions

1. Bacon slices should be used to cover or wrap the chopped turkey breast.
2. Using a crockpot, mix tomatoes, bay leaves, salt, black pepper, and garlic powder.
3. Afterwards, put the wrapped chopped turkey breast into the cooker, then, cover, and cook in the desired time, you can high cook for 4 hours or medium cook for 6 hour or low cook for 8 hours.
4. Take out the bay leaves from the prepared sauce. Then, turkey can be served in slices with the sauce.

Low-Carb Candied Yams with Marshmallows

Yields: 12 servings (1 cup) Overall Time: 35 minutes

Recipes:

One medium size pumpkin (Hokkaido 900 gram/pounds)

One and half sticks of unsalted butter (170 gram)

Not so required: 5-10 drops of liquid Stevia or 2 tablespoons of Erythritol or any other preferred healthy low-carb sweetener.

Directions:

1. Heat up the oven to 200 degrees Celsius or 400 degrees Fahrenheit. Ensure the pumpkin is peeled, deseeded and also diced into small cubes. Transfer in a clean pot filled with hot water and boil for approximately 10 minutes.
2. Afterwards, drain the water and transfer into a clean baking bowl. Add the butter, and then place the pumpkin into the oven for approximately 15 minutes. After that is done, take out from the oven then put aside.
3. Ramekins can also be used in small quantities for personal servings. It isn't required to use any

sweetener (as for me), but if desired you can decide to add a few drops of stevia to the pumpkin or some erthritol to the Pumpkin.

For the marshmallow:

1. Apply marshmallow cream to the pumpkin then spread equally.
2. Afterwards, Place the pumpkin with marshmallow cream under a broiler for approximately 10 minutes. Although, time may vary depending on your type of oven. I recommend you watch occasionally until it begins to appear brown. The marshmallow topping burns so quickly if it stays longer can required even if it's a minute.
3. When it is all done, take out from the oven. You can decide to serve warm or cold or just as desired. It

can even be reheated if needed. It can also be stored in the refrigerator for up to 5 days.

Keto Mashed Cauliflower

Recipes:

- Two medium heads of cauliflower
- Two tablespoons of olive oil
- Pepper (as desired)
- Half teaspoon of garlic powder
- 1/4 teaspoon onion powder
- Four ounces of cream cheese

- Two tablespoons of salted butter
- 1/4 cup sour cream
- One cup of sharp cheddar (shredded)
- 4 slices of bacon (cooked and crumbled)
- One stalk of green onion (sliced)
- Salt (as desired)

Directions

1. Heat up the oven to 400 degrees Fahrenheit. Line a large baking sheet with parchment. The cauliflower should be chopped into small florets and transfer onto the clean baking sheet. Shower with some olive oil and then, sprinkle with garlic powder, pepper, onion powder and some salt. Using your clean hands, Mix the cauliflower to ensure it is evenly coated with the seasonings and oil.

2. Ensure you place the cauliflowers in a single layer then put into the oven and bake for about 25-30 minutes or pay attention till it starts to appear brown and get tender. Stir the cauliflower at intervals while cooking.

3. When it is done. Place the cauliflower into the food processor. Pulse for just about 45-60 seconds, scraping down the sides as needed. You can decide to pulse less for a more textured mash or pulse longer for a more puree-like steadiness.

4. Break the cream cheese into pieces in a large clean container, then, put the butter to the clean container and microwave for about 30 seconds. Occasionally stir until it smoothens then add cheddar the sour cream. For the cheese to be melted you would have to microwave for another 30 seconds. Stir often till it smoothens.

5. Add the cauliflower into the container with the cheese mixture and softly mix together until it totally combined. Bend in green onion and bacon, you can reserve some garnish on top, if preferred.

6. Put into serving plate and garnish. Serve when it is warm.

Keto Pecan Pie Clusters

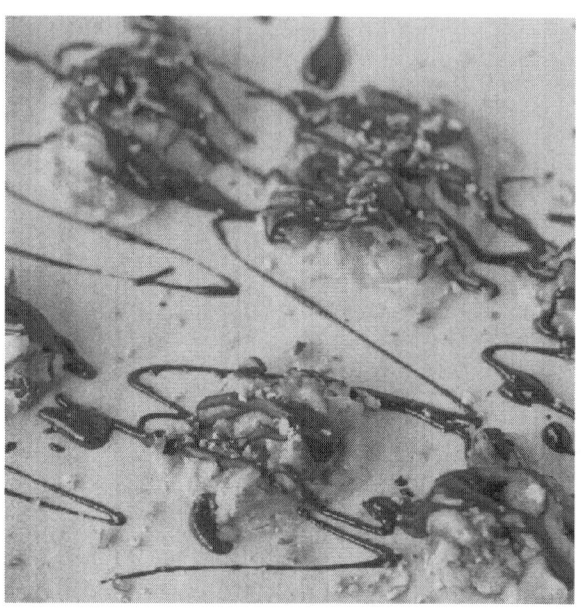

Recipes:

- A cup of sliced pecans
- Two ounce or 4 tablespoons of chopped dark chocolate or chopped sugar free chocolate
- Three tablespoons of butter
- 4 tablespoons of heavy cream

- 2 tablespoons of Zen Sweet (or a desired sweetener)
- 1 teaspoon of vanilla

Direction

1. Over moderate heat, heat up brown butter until it appears golden. Occasionally stir to avoid burning.

2. Once it appears golden, put heavy cream also whisk together. Reduce heat down to simmer.

3. Stirring swiftly, add vanilla also sweetener, ensure all lumps are broken.

4. Carry on stirring frequently for the next 5 minutes as the blend starts to thicken.

5. Blend will have consistency like to caramel and a little deepen. Take out from heat.

6. Blend in chopped pecans and spoon clusters onto either a parchment lined tray or a plate.

7. Put in a freezer for another 5 minutes.

8. Heat up dark chocolate in a microwave for about 20 to 40 seconds until it appears melted and becomes smoothen, afterwards, you can drizzle over clusters.

Keto Cornbread

Recipes:

- Half cup of almond flour
- 4 tablespoons of coconut flour
- One teaspoon of salt
- Half teaspoon of baking soda
- Three big eggs
- 8 tablespoons of heavy cream
- 4 tablespoons of butter melted

Optional Fillings:

- Two thinly sliced jalapeños
- 4 slices of cooked and crumbled bacon
- 8 tablespoons of shredded cheddar cheese

Directions

1. The oven should be preheated to 325 degrees Fahrenheit.
2. In an average clean container blend, all of the ingredients excluding the jalapeños (if you're not using toppings or some fillings just overlook them).
3. Transfer the batter into a 10.5-inches well-seasoned cast iron skillet and top with jalapeños, afterwards, bake for about 25 to 30 minutes. Let it cool for 5 minutes before beginning to cut and serve.

Keto Pumpkin Pie

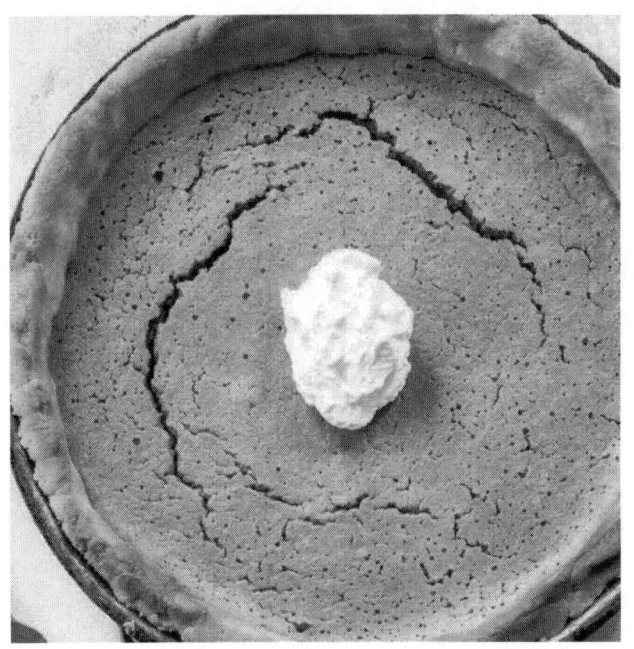

Total Time: 2 Hours 25 Minutes

Recipes:

Crust:

- One teaspoon of salt
- 2 2/3 cups of almond flour

- Three big eggs
- Six tablespoons of unsalted butter melted
- Six tablespoons of granulated Swerve erythritol

Filling:

- 15 ounces of unsweetened pumpkin puree (canned)
- 8 tablespoons of heavy cream
- Two big eggs
- One cup or 16 tablespoons of powdered Swerve erythritol
- One tablespoon pumpkin pie spice
- One teaspoon of vanilla extract
- One teaspoon of maple flavoring

Directions

For the crust:

1. Heat up oven to 325 degrees Fahrenheit and freely grease a 10.5-inches cast iron skillet with some butter.
2. In an average clean container blend, all the ingredients together until a thick ball of dough appears. Massage 2 or 3 times until it smoothens. Press the dough into the skillet and then bake for about 12 to 15 mins.

For the filling:

1. In an average container blend all filling ingredients. Transfer the blend into the pie crust, the pie edges should be covered with foil to avoid burning, then, bake 35 to 40 mins. Serve when it is totally cool.

Keto Scalloped Turnips

Yields: 12 Servings Total Time: 1 Hour 30 Minutes

Recipes:

- 4 tablespoons of divided unsalted butter
- 8 tablespoons of onion (minced)
- One tablespoon of fresh thyme (minced)
- 8 ounces cream cheese
- A cup of heavy cream

- A teaspoon of salt
- 1/4 teaspoon of fresh pepper
- Four cups of turnips (peeled & thinly sliced) Approximately 6 medium or small turnips.

Directions

1. Heat up oven to 350 degrees Fahrenheit.
2. Heat one tablespoon of butter in a 10-inches or bigger cast-iron skillet over moderate heat. Put in the onion plus thyme, then, cook occasionally stirring for about 5 mins until it becomes softened and beginning to appear brown. Take away and put aside.
3. In a heatproof container dissolve, the cream cheese, heavy cream, and salt and pepper together until it becomes smoothened.

4. Place a layer of turnips in the clean skillet but overlapping a little, place a few cubes of butter on top and sprinkle with a bit of the onion. Do the same with two layers more.
5. Put the cream sauce over the top and then cover with foil. Bake at 350 degrees Fahrenheit for about 30 minutes, afterwards, uncover and then bake for additional 45 minutes until the top turns golden.

Lemon Garlic Salmon

Overall Time: 25 minutes

Recipes:

- 1/4 cup of ghee or butter
- 6 to 8 garlic (cloves minced)
- 1/4 cup of chicken broth
- 1/4 cup of fresh lemon juice
- Sea salt
- One tablespoon of avocado oil

- Four salmon filets (around 6 ounces each), patted very dry
- Black pepper (Freshly cracked) if wanted
- Two tablespoons of fresh parsley (minced)
- Fresh lemons for garnish (thinly sliced)

Directions

Make the lemon garlic sauce:

1. In a small clean saucepan, butter or ghee should be melted over average heat. Afterwards, put the garlic and then sauté for just 1 to 2 minutes or until it begins to fragrant. Put in the lemon juice, chicken broth, and a few pinches of salt. Simmer the mixture until reduced by one third to half. The sauce will go from a very thin liquid to a thicker liquid, more bubble boil. Take away from heat then put away.

Make the salmon:

1. Take out the salmon filets from the refrigerator 10 to 20 minutes before starting to cook. Sprinkle both sides of the salmon filets abundantly with salt and then season with black pepper (freshly cracked), if wanted. Heat up the avocado oil in a clean large saucepan over average to high heat until it begins to shimmer.

2. Salmon filets should be carefully placed with skin side up and then cook until it appears slightly browned on bottom, for approximately 2 to 3 minutes or until it is crispy. Using a spatula carefully flip the salmon filets be careful not to peel off any flesh. Cook the other side of the salmon filets for about 3 to 4 minutes or until its skin begins to crisp and flesh starts to appear firm to touch. Take away at this point for a salmon cooked

around average. Keep cooking until flesh can be easily flake using a fork for a well-prepared salmon.

3. Take out pan from the heat and then add the lemon garlic sauce over. If desired you can sprinkle with parsley and also arrange lemon slices over. Serve with skin or you can easily remove with a spoon & serve with more lemon garlic sauce and lemon slices from the pan.

Note

If you want prefer to cook at medium-rare or medium temperature, you might try cooking the flesh side of the salmon only 1 to 2 mins then flipping and also cooking another 2 to 3 minutes. If you like well-prepared salmon, cook for 3 minutes on the flesh side and 4 minutes on the skin side, or until the flesh feels very firm and flakes easily using a fork.

Ensure you pat your salmon filets very dry on both sides using paper towels. This will aid the salmon to cook rapidly and equally, will promote a nice crust, and will avoid sticking to the pan.

Mini Pumpkin Cheesecake Tarts

Yields: 10 servings

Recipes:

Crust

- Half cup of salted butter
- Two big eggs
- ¾ cup of coconut flour
- Two tablespoons of Splenda (granulated)

Pumpkin Cheesecake Filling

- Six ounces of cream cheese, softened
- Three big eggs
- 1 ¼ cups of pumpkin puree
- ¾ cup of Splenda (granulated)
- One teaspoon of cinnamon
- One teaspoon of allspice
- One teaspoon of vanilla extract
- Half teaspoon of ground ginger

Directions:

Crust:

1. Put eight tablespoons of room butter, which is at room temperature, two eggs, and two tablespoons of Splenda into a clean mixing container.
2. Beat them well until the mixture turns liquid.

3. Afterwards, mix in the coconut flour gently. Continue until it gets to a pliable texture. Add in some of the saran wrap and then put it in the refrigerator for 20 to 30 mins.
4. Bring out the dough from the refrigerator. Then, you should squish the dough out onto some parchment paper.
5. Roll out the dough brought out of the refrigerator with the aid of a rolling pin until it is around ¼-inch thick.

Pumpkin Cheesecake Filling:

1. Place the 6 ounces block of cream cheese into a clean mixing container.
2. Beat properly until it becomes creamed.
3. In another clean container, blend one teaspoon of Allspice, half teaspoon of Ground Ginger. 3/4 Cup Splenda, and One teaspoon of Cinnamon together.

4. Pumpkin puree should be added to the cream cheese and then beat all together.
5. Add your sugar/spice mixture and eggs to the cream cheese and mix well.

The Marriage:

1. Heat up your oven to 400 degrees Fahrenheit.
2. Fill up the cupcake tin with the dough as much as you desire.
3. Place them into the oven for approximately 5 to 6 mins or until the edges start to turn golden brown.
4. Set oven to 350 degrees Fahrenheit.
5. Having done that, fill up the pastry shells with the pumpkin cheesecake blend, Make it nearly full.
6. Take out from the cupcake tray and let it cool.

Low-Carb Raspberry Baked Brie

Yields: 4 servings Overall Time: 30 minutes

Recipes:

- One cup plus two teaspoon shredded mozzarella (128 g/ 4.5 oz) - use low-moisture, part-skim, shredded mozzarella cheese; not fresh mozzarella.
- Half cup of almond flour (50 g/ 1.8 oz)
- One-wheel brie cheese (200 g/ 7.1 oz)
- Two tablespoons of Low-Carb Raspberry Chia Jam (40 g/ 1.4 oz)

Optional: 1 to 2 tablespoons of crumbled walnuts

Directions

1. Cook the Low-Carb Raspberry Chia Jam or any other use any low-carb jam you desire.
2. Heat up the oven to 360-degree Fahrenheit. Put the shredded mozzarella in another clean container and then microwave for about 50 to 70 seconds, checking occasionally, or you can also melt on the stove over a low heat. Afterwards, the almond flour should be mixed in.
3. Using a fork, stir well until a dough is created.
4. Roll the dough then you should cut between 2 sheets of parchment paper until large enough to wrap around the brie. The brie should be placed in the centre of the dough and also top with the chia jam. You can add crumbled walnuts if desired.

5. Afterwards, the dough should be wrapped around the cheese to make a parcel and pinch using your fingers to close.

6. Put in the oven and then bake for about 15 to 18 mins, or until it starts to appear golden brown on top.

7. Take away from the oven and let it cool for about 5 mins before starting to cut. You should eat straightaway while it is still warm.

Roasted Brussels Sprouts Salad with Mustard Basil Vinaigrette

Recipes:

For the Salad:

- One pound of brussels sprouts (stems removed) and also sliced into half
- One tablespoon of avocado oil or maybe olive oil
- Salt (A pinch)
- Four cups arugula
- Half cup of marinated artichokes (liquid drained)
- One-third cup of almonds chopped

For the dressing:

- Half cup of avocado oil or maybe olive oil
- Two tablespoons of dijon mustard
- Two tablespoons of balsamic vinegar
- One teaspoon of ground mustard
- Two cloves garlic (minced)
- ¼-teaspoon of sea salt
- ¼-teaspoon fresh cracked pepper
- ¼-cup of fresh basil leaves loosely packed

Directions

1. Heat up the oven to 400 degrees Fahrenheit. Lubricate a baking sheet using a cooking spray. Cover with brussels sprouts, and then coat the Brussels lightly with oil and sprinkle with little salt. Move to the oven and then bake for 15 mins.

2. As the Brussels are roasting, make the dressing. In a food processor or maybe a blender, combine oil, pepper, vinegar, ground mustard, fresh basil leaves, garlic, sea salt, and mustard. Blend till it smoothens.

3. Assemble the salad with artichoke hearts and arugula. Once the Brussels are okay and toasty, take out from the oven. Top salad with the Brussels. Pour in about half cup of the dressing (you should keep the rest for another usage). Toss to combine recipes and top with almonds.

Perfect Deviled Eggs with Bacon

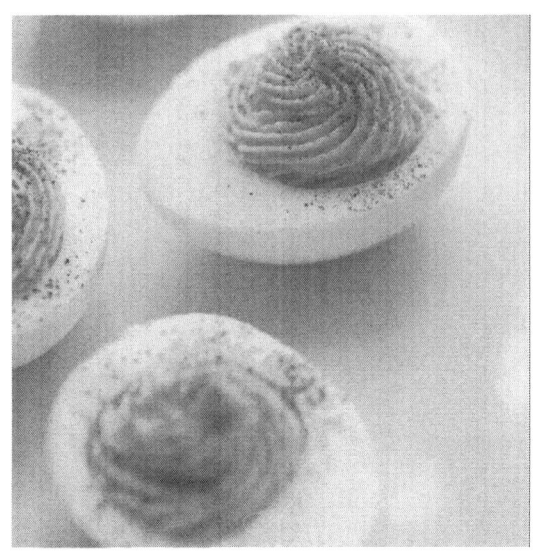

Yields: 6 servings **Overall Time:** 10 minutes

Recipes:

- Six hard-boiled eggs
- One teaspoon of Dijon mustard
- Half teaspoon of white vinegar
- 1/4 cup of mayonnaise
- Half to One tablespoon of butter softened or ghee
- Half teaspoon of salt

- Smoked paprika (to be used for sprinkling)
- Half slice of bacon (thinly cut), should be cooked until it is crisp, and well drained

Required Equipment:

- Open star tip (optional)
- Piping bag (optional)

Directions

1. This recipe is very easy to increase or reduce in quantity as necessary. Use the recipes above as your opening. See Note B for quantities for 1 dozen eggs.

2. Cut eggs into half using a sharp knife.

3. All yolks should be removed then transferred into a clean small container. Use a fork to mash until the yolks texture becomes small, consistent crumbs. The egg becomes smoother the more you mash, the smoother the final deviled egg.

4. Mix in softened butter, white vinegar, Dijon mustard, salt and mayonnaise. Bend to desired taste, by adding more salt, vinegar and mayonnaises.

5. Move the mixture to a wide-open star tip or piping bag fitted with a round. Pipe yolk mixture into egg whites in a swirl shape. Alternately, simply evenly spoon the yolk mixture into egg whites.

6. Top with a sprinkle of smoked paprika and 1-2 small pieces of bacon.

How to store

1. You can serve the filled deviled eggs straightaway. York filling can be made about a day earlier but you shouldn't pipe or fill the egg whites till a few minutes before serving, for best outcome. Leftovers can be stored in a refrigerator in an airtight container for a day or two.

Note

For hard-boiled eggs to be perfect, try this method:

1. Pour sufficient water in a clean saucepan, water should cover the eggs. Ensure the saucepan can fill the eggs just in one layer. Add pinches of salt and any kind of vinegar (a glug). Then boil.

2. While water is boiling, put eggs into the saucepan then set the timer for about 12 mins.

3. Move the eggs into an ice bath straightaway. Leave in the ice bath for about 5 mins to make sure it is very cool.

4. Ice bath should be drained. Strongly shake the container or pan that contains the boiled eggs against the sides of the container or pan and also against one another. When hard boiled eggs are well cracked, ensure you peel the eggs in running water so as to removed stocked shell.

Note

For twelve eggs, you will need the following quantities:

- A dozen of hard-boiled eggs
- Two teaspoons of Dijon mustard
- One teaspoon of white vinegar
- Half cup of mayonnaise
- One to Two tablespoons of softened butter
- Salt (a teaspoon)
- For sprinkling get smoked paprika
- A slice bacon (should be cut into thin pieces also cooked until it is crisp, and well drained)

Note

To prepare these deviled eggs Whole30 ensure you sure Dijon mustard, mayonnaise, and bacon are compliant. Ensure you use ghee not butter.

Keto Pumpkin Seed Bread

Yields: <u>10</u> Slices Overall Time: 55 mins

Recipes:

- Half cup of <u>pumpkin seeds</u> pepita
- Half cup of <u>butter</u> melted
- Five large eggs
- <u>Salt</u> (a teaspoon)
- Two cups of <u>almond flour</u>
- Half teaspoon of <u>xanthan gum</u>

Directions

1. Isolate yolks from the egg whites. Then, beat the egg whites until they have formed white peaks.
2. In the same container, place the xanthan gum, egg yolks, melted butter, salt, almond flour and xanthan gum.
3. Then you should mix till it is well joined.
4. Afterwards, pour it into a well-greased (9" X 5") loaf tin.
5. On the top of the mix, pour the pepita seeds.
6. Bake at 355 degrees Fahrenheit for 45 minutes (fan forced).
7. Slice it to, then serve to enjoy.

Slow Cooker Pumpkin Cheddar Soup with Chorizo

Yields: **6** servings **Overall Time:** 4 hrs 5 mins

Recipes:

- Half of onion (minced)
- ¼- teaspoon of chipotle powder (or as desired)
- Pumpkin puree (15 ounce canned)
- Half teaspoon of salt

- One-pound of chorizo or any other preferred spicy sausage cooked and also crumbled
- Half teaspoon of cumin
- Half teaspoon of garlic powder
- ¼- teaspoon of black pepper
- Four cups of chicken broth (preferably homemade)
- Six-ounces of a sharp cheddar cheese (grated)
- Salt and pepper to taste

Directions

1. Add chicken broth, pumpkin puree, onion, salt, cumin, chipotle powder, pepper, and garlic powder to a clean big slow cooker. Stir it well and then cook on low for approximately 4 hrs or on high approximately 2 hrs.

2. Put shredded cheese & then let it melt, afterwards blend soup with an immersion blender or food processor (this might require you to work in bits) or you can move to a big clean blender.
3. You should spoon into containers and then you sprinkle each with some chorizo.
4. This recipe can also be made on a stove, a stockpot or in a clean big saucepan. You would only simmer the recipes from the first procedure for about 20 mins or there about before putting the cheese and blending it.

Stuffed Pork Tenderloin and Roasted Radish

Yields: 5 servings

Recipes:

For the Roast:

- Two pounds of Pork Tenderloin
- One and a half tsp. of Onion Powder
- Two teaspoons of Rosemary

- Three teaspoons of Salt
- One teaspoon of Garlic Powder
- One teaspoon of Pepper
- Two teaspoons of Thyme

The Stuffing:

- One-pound of Ground Pork Sausage
- Three-ounces of Spinach
- Half teaspoon of Thyme
- Salt and Pepper to Taste
- ¼-teaspoons of Garlic Powder
- Six-ounces of Baby Bella Mushrooms
- Half teaspoon of Rosemary
- ¼-teaspoons of Onion Powder

The Roast Radish:

- One teaspoon of Rosemary
- 16-ounces of Red Radish
- Salt and Pepper to Taste
- Four tablespoons of Duck Fat

Directions:

1. Season sides of the pork with pepper, garlic powder, rosemary, thyme, salt and onion powder while the pork tenderloin is butterflied.
2. The mushrooms should be sliced and heat up the oven to 400 degrees Fahrenheit.
3. You would have to cook the sausage over moderate heat. As soon as the sausage begins to turn brown, you should break it up with a spatula and seasoning then add the mushrooms. Afterwards, put the spinach to the pan for wilt just for a little while.

4. Pour the blend over the top of the pork tenderloin and you should then spread out equally. Wrap up the pork tenderloin with butchers netting or tie with twine. Cook this at 400 degrees Fahrenheit for about 50 to 60 mins or until the thermometer indicates 140 degrees Fahrenheit.
5. You would need to slice the entire radish into halves and season then place into a bag with duck fat. Set aside while the pork is cooking.
6. As soon as the pork is well cooked, take out from the oven and turn oven to 450 degrees Fahrenheit. You should then roast the radish for about 30 mins while the pork tenderloin is wrapped in foil to rest.
7. Serve when hot to enjoy.

Sweet 'N Tangy Cranberry Relish

Overall Time: 40 Mins

Recipes:

- 1/3- cups of white wine vinegar
- One finely chopped rosemary spring
- ½ to ¾ - cups of allulose or erythritol xylitol (as desired)
- One-pound of cranberries

- One medium finely minced banana shallot (abt 50 grams)

Directions

1. Put sweetener and vinegar into a clean saucepan over a low heat or a medium, occasionally stirring till it is totally dissolved and just simmering. After that, Add rosemary, shallot and the cranberries. Reduce the heat to low, then cover (ensure you leave it a bit ajar), and then you simmer for about 20 to 25 mins you should stir occasionally, until it becomes syrupy and thicken.
2. You can to taste it at about 15 minute and also adjust the sweetness as required. You can keep in a refrigerator in an airtight bowl for four to five days and in a freezer for up to 3 months.

Roasted Turkey Leg

Yields: 4 Servings

Recipes:

- One-pound each Two Turkey Legs (bones removed)
- One teaspoon of Liquid Smoke
- ¼-teaspoon of Cayenne Pepper
- Half teaspoon of Dried Thyme

- Salt (Two teaspoons)
- Half teaspoon of Garlic Powder
- Half teaspoon of Pepper
- One teaspoon of Worcestershire
- Two tablespoons of peanut oil or Duck Fat or any other preferred animal fat
- Half teaspoon of Onion Powder
- Half teaspoon of Ancho Chili Powder

Directions

1. Stir all dry recipes in a clean small container. Afterwards, add all the wet recipes then blend all together. Turkey legs should be patted totally dry and season well.
2. Heat the oven to 350 degrees Fahrenheit. On a <u>cast iron skillet</u> bring two teaspoons of fat then medium to high heat. As soon as the smoke from the oil is noticed, gently put the patted dry turkey legs into the pan afterwards sear on each side for 1 to 2 mins.
3. Put in the oven at 350 degrees Fahrenheit for about 50 to 60 mins or until it is well cooked.
4. You can carry on to serve with your desired side dish.

Easy Garlic Butter Herb Roasted Turkey

Yields: 12 Servings Overall Time: 3 hrs 10 mins

Recipes:

- Two gallons of Water

- Two and a half cups of Kosher salt

- A twelve-pounds Whole turkey

- Half cup of softened Butter (you can use ghee if you want a dairy-free, Whole30. paleo)

- One tablespoon of finely chopped fresh sage
- One tablespoon of chopped finely Fresh rosemary
- One tablespoon of Fresh thyme (leaves only)
- Four cloves of minced Garlic
- One teaspoon of Lemon zest
- Half tablespoon of Sea salt
- Half tablespoon of fresh Black pepper

Directions:

For the Turkey Brine:

1. Stir together two and a half cups (128 grams) of kosher salt and two gallons (7.5 Liters) of water in a clean big stockpot big enough to accommodate the whole turkey. The whole turkey should be submerged in the brine, afterwards refrigerate for about 10 to twelve hrs.

2. Place the whole turkey into a clean roasting pan with a clean roasting rack after the turkey is brined, water drained and well patted dry.

For the Garlic Herb Butter Turkey Rub:

1. In a small clean container, crush together the sage, lemon zest, black pepper, minced garlic, the softened butter, sea salt, rosemary and thyme.
2. Separate the skin from the meat underneath using your hands under the turkey skin. ((Do this gently to avoid tearing of the skin)
3. Half of the butter should be spread all over the turkey beneath the skin afterwards spread the over the skin the other half of the butter.

For Roast Turkey:

1. Put the oven rack in the middle. Afterwards, Heat the oven to 350 degrees Fahrenheit.

2. Put the turkey into the oven then roast. For a 12-pounds turkey which is uncovered it will take 45 mins while covered will take about 2 1/4 hrs. You can easily cover with foil before putting into the oven.

3. Confirm that the turkey is ready with the thermometer. The thermometer should indicate 165 degrees for the best option. Target 150 to 155 degrees Fahrenheit for a juicy turkey, and then cover in foil straightaway after taking it out from the oven. You should let the turkey rest while it is still covered in foil, for approximately 20 min it will be about 165 to 170 degrees before starting.

Low Carb Creamed Spinach with Cream Cheese

Yields: 4 Servings Overall Time: 15 minutes

Recipes:

- Three tablespoons of Butter
- Half cup of Heavy cream
- Ten-ounces of chopped Baby spinach (abt 16 cups)
- Four minced Garlic cloves

- Three-ounces of Cream cheese (small pieces)
- 1/4 teaspoon of fresh Black pepper
- One teaspoon of Italian seasoning
- 1/4 teaspoon of Sea salt
- You can use Parmesan cheese for topping if desired

Directions

1. Heat up the butter in a big clean sauté pan over a moderate heat. Afterwards, add in the garlic then sauté till it begins to scent.
2. Sauté for two to four mins after adding the spinach until it is wilted. Cover for one to two minutes, if the pan is so filled to stir, this will wilt the spinach at the bottom. You can stir in a folding motion afterwards.

3. Add in Italian seasoning, cream cheese, heavy cream, black pepper and sea salt. Constantly stir till the cream cheese totally melts, afterwards, you will cook until it thickens.

Note

If wanted you can sprinkle in Parmesan cheese then serve to enjoy.

Conclusion

This Keto Christmas Cookbook will give you amazing ideas to add a delicious twist to both modern and traditional recipes.

The recipes are adequate for all cooking skill levels and are great to prepare with the families. Bring the best of dishes to your home.

Have fun and enjoy your Christmas!

Printed in Dunstable, United Kingdom